Volume Eleven

HOW TO COMPETE

Volume Eleven

HOW TO COMPETE

Curtis J. Badger

STACKPOLE
BOOKS

Published by
STACKPOLE BOOKS
5067 Ritter Road
Mechanicsburg, PA 17055

Printed in Hong Kong

10 9 8 7 6 5 4 3 2 1

First edition

Cover design by Mark Olszewski
Interior design by Marcia Lee Dobbs

Library of Congress Cataloging-in-Publication Data
(Revised for vol. 11)

Badger, Curtis J.
   Bird-carving basics

   Contents: v. 1. Eyes — [etc.] — v. 4 Bills and
beaks — [etc.] — v. 9 Tools — — v. 11. How to
compete.
   1. Wood-carving.   2. Birds in art.   I. Title.
TT199.7.B33   1990   731'.832   90-9491
   ISBN 0-8117-2334-8 (v.1)

Contents

Foreword

In working on the Bird Carving Basics series over the past three years, I've discovered a few General Truths about carvers and carving. Foremost is that the more talented the carver, the more generous he or she is when it comes to sharing information and insights with others. I suppose someone who is really good is too confident to feel threatened when a beginning carver quizzes him on eye insertion techniques or texturing style.

The best artists, it seems to me, realize that learning carving is like learning a language. Once you master the technical skills, then you can begin to communicate. Mastery of skills does not an artist make. First there must be something you want to say, and then you must be able to successfully communicate your thoughts.

You can learn carving skills through books such as this or in seminars with experienced carvers, but to be successful in carving competitions you must use those skills to make a statement all your own. Previous books in this series have shown how leading artists go about the technical aspects of carving; this volume deals more with the creative process, especially as it pertains to the world of carving competitions.

The artists included in this book are all winners. Some of them are world champions; all have won many ribbons at competitions across the United States and Canada. These top carvers explain why they enter competitions, what it takes to win, and how to push the carving process beyond the ordinary.

Our hope is that by studying earlier volumes of Bird Carving Basics and attending workshops, you have gained the rudimentary carving skills. And now, in reading the comments of top artists and looking at photographs of their work, we hope you will be inspired to enter competitions, learn from the work of other competitors, and use your skills to say something to us about birds and flight.

I want to thank all of the carvers who agreed to be interviewed for this book and who allowed me to use photos of their work. I've learned a lot from them, and I hope you will too. Thanks, too, to Cathy Hart, editor of *Wildfowl Carving & Collecting* magazine, who loaned photos from the magazine files. Thanks to Dan Williams, who is not only a talented carver but an outstanding photographer as well, for many of the photos of competition winners.

Introduction

Carving competitions have been around for a long time. A half-century ago some of the best decoy makers in the country would get together in New York at the National Decoy Show to compare their wares, with a friendly bit of competition added to make the weekend interesting. Those who brought home blue ribbons might possibly have found reason to raise their prices a few pennies.

The character of bird carving competitions has changed in recent years. The work is no longer limited to hunting decoys; indeed, in many of the major competitions the so-called "decoratives" dominate.

In addition, the stakes are greater. While in the 1940s carvers competed mainly for ribbons, today the prize money can reach several thousand dollars. The largest competition in the country, the Ward World Championship held each April in Ocean City, Maryland, offers a total purse of about $80,000, with the top prize a $20,000 purchase award for the best entry in the decorative lifesize category. The competition is sponsored by the nonprofit Ward Foundation of Salisbury, Maryland, which operates the Ward Museum of Wildfowl Art. The foundation was named for the late Steve and Lem Ward, pioneer wildfowl carvers from the Eastern Shore of Maryland.

The quality and style of the work have also changed in recent years. In the early 1970s carvers discovered rotary cutting tools and pyrographic instruments that enabled them to capture extremely fine detail. In talented hands these instruments can create a wooden feather indistinguishable to the human eye from the real thing.

So bird carving, and the carving competitions, set out along two paths, one followed by the classic decoy maker, the other by those who preferred the more decorative, realistic birds intended for the display case rather than the duck blind.

Carving competitions are still divided along the two paths, but it is an agreeable division, a matter of personal taste and motivation rather than an evolution from "crude" decoys to the "fine art" of decoratives. Most competitions today offer contests featuring both gunning decoys and decoratives, so it's not unusual to go to a show and see exquisite little chickadees displayed alongside black ducks fitted with decoy weights and anchors.

The competitions tend to be very democratic— carvers of all persuasions and abilities are welcome. Entering one of the contests is something like running in a marathon: you can share the same arena with the best in the world, and you don't have to feel bad about not finishing first.

Most competitions include categories that reflect varying degrees of expertise. Usually there are novice, intermediate, and open or professional categories, so those who enter will be competing against others of similar experience and ability. Cash awards are usually given at the professional level, while the novice and intermediate winners get trophies and ribbons.

Competitions also cater to a wide variety of tastes and approaches to carving. In most, you'll find a contest for traditional gunning decoys, one for highly detailed decorative birds, another for miniature carvings, and, increasingly, a contest featuring a more free-form approach often called interpretive sculpture.

If you've been carving for a while and you'd like to test your skills against those of others, a carving competition is the logical forum. Before you enter, it would be a good idea to attend a contest or two and get an idea of the quality of work being entered. If you feel you're ready to step into the fray, by all means do so.

Competitions should build confidence and spark creativity. At the larger contests, several hundred carvers enter, so the exposure to so many carvers and carvings should inspire you. If you see a particular bird that intrigues you, talk to the artist about it. Most competitors are very generous with technical information and are willing to help beginners.

In the event you don't come home with a ribbon, don't despair. Use the competition as an educational experience. Most judges are fellow carvers and artists, so after the contest ask them what they considered the strengths and weaknesses of your work. Most carving competitions are organized by carvers themselves and are intended to bring together people who share a passion for birds and bird art. The intention is to share information and ideas, not simply to dole out ribbons.

The best approach is to play down the competitive aspects. If you win, that's great. If you don't get a ribbon, don't worry about it. Learn what you can do to improve. Ask questions of more experienced carvers. Resolve to make your work even better, and come back next time and try again.

Competitions can instruct and encourage carvers. They can put your work before the buying public. They can help build careers in wildlife art. They can foster friendships that will last a lifetime. As in many pursuits, what you get out of carving competitions is fairly proportional to what you put in.

This book presents a carver's view of competitions. We asked some of the best artists in the field how and why they started competing, why they continue, and what they do to make their work stand out from the rest. We hope their insights, and their work, will encourage you to enter, to strive to improve your technique, and to continue the tradition of sharing and teaching.

1

Why Compete?

Whether you're ready to enter carving competitions depends on your attitude as well as on the quality of your work. How fragile is your ego? Can you take criticism? Can you enjoy the contest whether or not you win a ribbon?

Some of us are more competitive than others, and some of us are more sensitive than others. Would not winning a contest throw you into a fit of anger and depression and encourage you to sell your carving tools and take up scuba diving? Would a blue ribbon so inflate your ego that you wouldn't be fit to live with for the next year?

Most of the carvers who enter competitions realize that when the ribbons are awarded, it simply means that two of the three judges preferred a particular piece. They avoid emotional extremes whether they win or lose. They attend and enter because they enjoy the fellowship with other carvers, they enjoy seeing what other artists are doing, and they know the major competitions attract collectors who have their checkbooks at the ready. Many carvers can count on picking up a few sales or commissions during the weekend of contests, and if they win a ribbon or some cash—then that's a bonus.

Ernie Muehlmatt of Springfield, Pennsylvania, has what most would consider a healthy attitude toward competitions. He has entered the Ward World Championship nearly every year for the past two decades and has won the prestigious competition three times, twice for miniatures and once for a lifesize carving. "I only enter the Ward now, and I do it just for

These Steller's jays by Ernie Muehlmatt took a
third in the Ward competition in 1985. The effects
of competitions are cumulative, says Ernie,
helping over time to establish an artist's
reputation.

Competitions are popular with carvers, collectors, and the general public. The Ward Foundation's annual World Championship draws more than two thousand entries and several thousand spectators.

fun," he says. "I'm not a really competitive person, but I like to beat guys who are good."

The advantage of competitions in marketing one's work is a cumulative process, most carvers agree. A single win does not bring fame and fortune, and not receiving a ribbon doesn't mean you're on the road to ruin. The most successful carvers, like Ernie, are the ones who have put together an impressive record over a period of time.

"The effect of competitions on a carver's career comes in steps," he says. "If you win or finish well a few times, it gives you credibility. In my case, it allowed me to write a book on carving that sold well. And then the book helped attract students to my workshops. It all goes hand in hand."

Carvers are not advised to sit by the phone waiting for calls from collectors after one win. When Ernie won his first World Championship, he expected a bull market for his carvings, but it didn't materialize. "It's ironic, but I finally figured out that when you win, collectors feel that either your work is out of reach financially or you're booked up until the next century. The three times I won were the loneliest times in my career. No one called."

The competitions should primarily be fun and educational, says Ernie. "It's a good forum to show off your work. Even if you don't get a ribbon, you can still sell your carvings. It's stimulating to compete with others and see what they're doing. It's a great learning experience. I tried doing one-piece carvings after seeing the work of Barbara Nelson and Greg Woodard at the Ward show, and now I feel it's the only way to go. You can carve the bird and the habitat as one piece, and it's like painting on a blank canvas. It's a combination of flat art and sculpture."

Accelerate the Learning Curve

Ernie Muehlmatt began carving and entering shows and competitions following a twenty-year career in the family florist business, but in recent years some carvers have gone directly from art school to full-time careers, thanks at least in part to carving competitions. Larry Barth entered his senior thesis project at Carnegie Mellon University in the Ward World Championship in 1979 and finished second. Encouraged by his success, he began a full-time career in wood sculpting after graduation.

"I had been carving for a long time, but I'd been doing it in virtual isolation until I went to my first competition," Larry says. "During the summer after my high school graduation we passed through the Eastern Shore on a family trip. The posters for the World Championship were still up, so we decided to come back the next year and see what it was all about."

His first trip to a carving competition was pivotal in Larry's career. Although he had been sketching and carving birds since his early teens, he didn't realize so many other people were involved—or that the quality

Larry won a first in shorebirds at the open level at the 1991 Ward competition with this spotted sandpiper. *(Dan Williams photo)*

of work was so high. "I was just floored," he says of his first competition. "I had no idea what was going on in the carving world. I was carving on my own, at my own pace, picking up the technical things by myself. I knew I had the ability, but it hadn't occurred to me to take it as far as these carvers had done. I got tremendously excited about it—really fired up—and I couldn't wait to go home and get to work."

The next year Larry entered three pieces in the novice class and won first, second, and third in show. "I suddenly realized I could make a living in bird carving. I knew what I wanted to do for the rest of my life."

Accuracy and attention to detail are compulsory in carving competitions. This close-up of Larry's sandpiper shows impeccable detail. The head and eyes are the focal point of a carving, says Larry, and these areas require special attention. *(Dan Williams photo)*

The personality of the bird is in the eyes, Larry believes, and he proves it with this carving of a shrike, which won the Ward World Championship in 1991. *(Dan Williams photo)*

Larry has won the $20,000 top prize for decorative lifesize sculpture at the Ward four times, and he continues to enter competitions. "For me the competitions accelerated the learning curve," he says. "I was able to pick up the technical information much more quickly. And I still like attending and competing. It keeps me on my toes, and I enjoy seeing what others are doing. Competitions are the best forum bird carving has. It's a clearinghouse, a place where everything comes to a head."

As far as marketing his work, Larry agrees with Ernie Muehlmatt that the effect of competitions is cumulative. "In my experience, getting one blue ribbon is not going to make a carver's work salable, but over time, success in competitions will help."

Larry advises beginning competitors to carve what they like rather than what they think the judges will like. "After finishing second with the great horned owls in 1979 I entered open class over the next two years and didn't get a blue. It was very frustrating. I was carving for the judges, making pieces I thought would win, but everyone else had the same ideas. It was an exercise in futility. So in 1982 I carved a loon for my wife and a fox sparrow for myself and entered them, and they both won. That was a very valuable lesson. Carve what's important to you, not what you think the judges will like."

A Confidence Booster

Floyd Scholz was a college decathlon champion in Connecticut before moving to Vermont in the early 1980s to give bird carving a try. Entering a crow in the amateur class of the 1981 U.S. National Decoy Show in New York helped in his decision to become a professional carver.

"I had carved a crow and had it on display at a friend's store in Connecticut," he says. "Eldredge Arnold, a well-known Connecticut carver, came in one day and noticed it and suggested I enter it in the U.S. Nationals. I decided to give it a shot, even though I thought I'd probably get laughed right out of the show. As it turned out, the crow won best in show in amateur class and got me really excited about carving. After attending the show for two days and studying the works of other carvers, I realized I was doing comparable work in total isolation and that if I really worked at it I could improve."

Floyd did improve—substantially. Today he is considered one of America's top sculptors of raptors and has won many competitions around the country. Exposure gained through the contests helped him market his work and gradually turn to carving as a full-time occupation. "As a beginning exhibitor, I made many contacts with collectors and other artists," he says. "This gave me the determination and encouragement to improve, because I love the art form and felt (and still do) that I have so much more to learn.

Floyd Scholz's carving career began when fellow carver Eldredge Arnold saw his work in a shop and urged him to enter the U.S. Nationals in New York. Floyd is now one of America's leading carvers of raptors. *(Tad Merrick photo)*

"If you are new to the art and are eager to get your name known, the various carving competitions are a great way to do that. I don't consider the shows themselves a great forum for marketing one's work, because they're usually stressful, crowded, and confusing affairs, so it's difficult for the artist and collector to get together and talk business. Winning consistently sure doesn't hurt one's marketability to the collectors who frequent shows, but most of my clients are fine arts collectors or business people who love art for art's sake and couldn't give a hoot what three judges have to say."

Floyd advises beginning carvers to take lessons and workshops with more experienced carvers but to develop their own style before entering competitions. "I encourage beginners to study the bird and make sure the size is correct. I think it's okay to take lessons to learn the techniques, but a student shouldn't copy someone else's work, especially if he's going to take it to a carving show or contest and enter it as his own."

Family Affair

No family has so dominated the world of decorative decoys as the Brunets of Galliano, Louisiana. Tan Brunet is a five-time world champion in decorative decoy pairs at the Ward. Tan's oldest son, Jett, has won the same award twice, and a second son, Jude, won in 1993. The Brunets, and their cousin and neighbor, Jimmie Vizier, have won all the major carving awards in the country—some more than once.

"The Vizier family influenced me long before we began entering the competitions," says Tan. "I watched Jimmie carve and learned from him, and he learned from his daddy, Odee Vizier, and his uncle, Cadis. In my late teens and early twenties I made decoys to hunt with; then when the plastic decoys came along there was a lull. I made cabinets and pirogues, some sculpture, and other wooden items. I was in the lumber business for thirty-five years, so I was used to working with wood. I did some decoys that I traded to friends or gave to family members. Around that time a magazine called *North American Decoys* came out— this was in the late sixties and early seventies. Through it we met other collectors and learned about some of the shows and competitions around the country. The magazine had photos of some beautiful decoys that were making the transition from hunting stools to mantel birds.

"I went to Easton, Maryland, for the Waterfowl Festival in 1974, and that's what opened the doors for me. Dr. Harry Walsh and Bill Perry, who ran the festival, took me under their wings and did a lot for me.

"I had sent birds in 1975 and 1976 to the Ward competition, and finally in 1977 I went and won best in world with a pair of pintails."

Tan later won four more Ward championships, plus two best in shows at the Ward, many best in shows at other competitions, a dozen head-whittling competitions, and the first Masters Class competition in Minnesota in 1989. In addition, his auction birds

Tan Brunet of Galliano, Louisiana, is a five-time world champion. His work, as demonstrated by this mallard hen, is simple and elegant and is based on the tradition of hunting decoys. *(Dan Williams photo)*

used by competitions as fund-raising items have fetched record prices. How have the competitions affected his career?

"They've done a lot for me. I've been in the magazines, on television shows, in carving books. Winning the competitions created a lot of exposure for me. You don't have to win every show, but consistency means a lot. If you're a consistent winner and are considered in the top echelon of the carving world, then it will help the market for your work."

For beginning carvers, Tan's advice is to master the basics of carving and painting before tackling complex projects. "My basic advice is start at the bot-

Jett Brunet is a two-time world champion who in 1989 won all three ribbons in the floating waterfowl category at the Ward competition. Jett displays his winning gadwall, pintail, and redhead.

tom, do your research, get a good pattern book—Pat Godin has the best—go to a class, and buy the carving books. There's a lot of good information out there."

Like Father . . .

Tan's eldest son, Jett, began carving when he was nine years old, and while he was in his early twenties he won his first Ward world championship. "My father was competing when I was growing up, and I went to all the shows with him and decided that I wanted to do the same thing. He was winning championships, and that really had an appeal for me—to have people look at your work and like it and want to buy it. I learned from the beginning the right way to get involved in competitions through my father."

Entering—and winning—competitions around the country has been central to Jett's success as an artist, and although he learned technique from his father, he quickly developed his own style and identity. "He used to be known as Tan Brunet's son. Now I'm known as Jett Brunet's dad," jokes Tan.

"The competitions made my father well known in the carving community, and they have done the same for me," says Jett. "Competing helped me find buyers for my work, and the more success you have the more valuable your work becomes. My father and I both quit

Jett's gadwall shows simple but very pleasant design and extraordinary detail and painting. *(Dan Williams photo)*

His redhead drake is carved in a more complex preening posture. *(Dan Williams photo)*

regular jobs and are carving full time, and the main reason is our success in competitions. Consistency is important. You don't have to win every time, but it's important to be involved and have high-quality work."

Like his dad, Jett recommends taking classes with established carvers. "They'll give you good advice. They'll show you the basic procedure of going from a block of wood to a decoy. But when you get into competitions you need to develop your own ideas. Put your own artistic feelings into it. Have your own style. If you are going to have a future in this business, your work is going to have to stand on its own. If you do good work, the ribbons will come."

Accustomed to Competition

Few carvers today have competed more in their lives than Jim Sprankle of Kent Island, Maryland. Jim was signed by the Dodgers out of high school and played professional baseball for ten years with the Dodgers and Redlegs organizations. Next came a career in business, then in 1976 he began his full-time involvement in wildfowl art. Jim has won hundreds of ribbons at competitions across the United States, he teaches seminars at his waterfront studio and around the country, and he markets his own line of carving supplies.

"Competing is something I've been doing all my life," he says. "I played baseball for many years, then was in business, so competing in bird carving didn't seem to be any different. Competitions are very positive. It's the quickest way I know of in bird art to get recognition. Winning is the ultimate, of course. I've always worked under the theory that I'd rather carve one or two good birds and be a winner than go to a show with a whole box full of carvings and have them get an honorable mention or nothing at all."

The relationship between blue ribbon winners and marketability is vividly illustrated in a story Jim tells of his experience at the 1984 Ward competition. He had carved seven birds and had sold all of them sight-unseen to collectors for delivery after the contest. He entered all in the competition; six won blue ribbons and the seventh a red. The collector who had agreed to purchase the seventh bird decided not to buy it but did take one of the blue-ribbon birds he had agreed to buy. "I think this shows the importance people put on first-place birds at major shows," says Jim.

Jim recommends that beginning carvers find their niche when they begin competing. "Many of the best carvers specialize," he says. "Some do raptors, songbirds, shorebirds, or waterfowl. I think it's difficult for a carver to be competitive if he's going to carve a songbird one day and a duck the next. You have to home in on something. If it's going to be waterfowl, then to stay competitive you'd better be very serious about waterfowl."

Jim follows his own advice, specializing in waterfowl. File cabinets bulge with photos and other reference material, an aviary is attached to his studio, and another cabinet is filled with taxidermy specimens. To carry the specialization theory even further, Jim advises competition carvers to learn to do one puddle duck and one diving duck really well. "After you win a few blue ribbons, then you want to go for the best in show awards [where the winning diving ducks compete against winning puddle ducks], and you don't want to have two of your diving ducks or two of your puddle ducks competing against each other."

An Environmental Statement

Leo Osborne of Joseph, Oregon, is one of America's most prolific, adventurous, and eclectic carvers. While the world of bird carving is generally seen as conservative, predictable, and infatuated with realism, Leo is full of surprises. Several years ago, when competitions introduced an interpretive category, it suited Leo perfectly. The interpretive label catches all the carving styles that fall through the gaps in the rules of the other divisions. Entries can be painted or not painted, realistic or not realistic, finely carved or roughed out with a chain saw.

Although Leo has been a consistent winner in bird carving competitions for several years, his contemporary work includes fish, mammals, and human figures. He works in bronze and clay as well as wood, and his work is usually characterized by a strong environmental conscience. Themes involving wildlife of the Pacific Northwest predominate in his most recent sculptures.

Leo got involved in competitions while living in Maine in the 1980s. He entered a carving in the U.S. Nationals in New York and won a ribbon, but he was most impressed by the number and quality of carvings entered. He then attended the Ward competition in Ocean City, Maryland, the following spring. "The Ward was just too much for me to comprehend," he says. "It blew my mind."

There were hundreds of competitors, more than one thousand carved birds, and an audience that packed the resort city's convention center. But Leo, whose art school background had not prepared him to approach sculpture as a competitive sport, was taken aback by the rules, the judging system, and the entrants' apparent determination to please the judges rather than create bird carvings with any degree of independence.

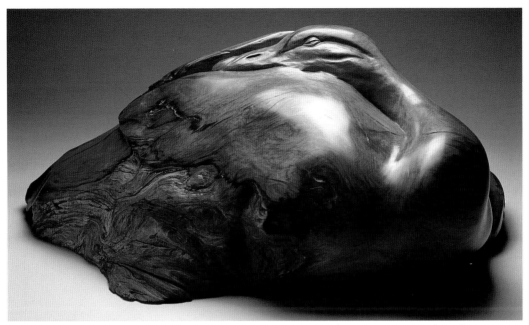

Leo Osborne carved this goose emerging from a redwood burl and titled the sculpture *Gentle Rest.* Leo is one of the top artists in the interpretive division, where carvers are allowed free rein when it comes to style and presentation.

"People were carving to compete," he says. "They weren't carving for artistic value or in the spirit of who they were as individuals, so quite frankly that turned me off to competitions, and I went away from that first year at the Ward competition never wanting to come back there again.

"I was new at carving birds, but I knew I didn't want to get involved in carving for a panel of judges. So I decided to compete just against myself, to become as good as I could be and try to get into some of the best exhibitions I could. Later, when I felt confident about what I was doing, I decided to go back into competitions. I was at the point where I was comfortable with my work, and I knew that nothing I heard from judges or peers would sway me from going in what I perceived as my own direction. That took two or three years.

Then I came back to the Ward competition with something that was unique and different, and whether I won or not I felt pleased with my work."

When Leo decided to re-enter competitions, he brought work that was, in the conservative context of bird carving, revolutionary. He made wall sculptures of swallows perched on a rocky ledge, and often he would hint at the presence of other birds by adding just a shadow somewhere on the wall. He carved bird and animal figures from redwood burls. "The first year I entered a wall sculpture in the Ward competition it won no ribbons at all, but *Wildfowl Carving & Collecting* magazine did its first Competition annual that year, and they included my piece, even though it didn't place, because it was so different. To me, that was better than winning first because it was being recognized as unique.

"The competitions gave me a chance to come in as a rebel—my work wasn't in the mainstream. So in an odd sort of way the competitions helped me promote the work I was doing. At that point in my career competing helped me market my work, but I think now the collectors who follow competitions are looking for decorative work, not the interpretives. I've had to go far beyond competitions to find a market. I've gone to galleries and museums to try to sell enough work to make a living. The prize money for interpretive sculpture is far less than for decoratives, and I find that unfortunate and hard to justify."

Leo advises beginning competitors to carve for themselves, not judges, and to strive to create work that is unique. "If I break a rule and my piece doesn't win, I don't care as long as the sculpture gets attention and is a good work of art. I'd rather have something that makes a statement than win a ribbon. A ribbon is only good for a year, and then someone else wins. But if your style and approach is unique and powerful and dynamic, that's going to last forever."

2

The Classes of Competition

The first time I attended a carving competition I was totally befuddled. It didn't help that my first competition was the Ward World Championship, which is held in Ocean City, Maryland, each April. The Ward is the largest competition in the world, and the resort's convention center was filled with more than two thousand carved birds displayed on tables running in great rows through the arena. Some wore ribbons and some didn't.

At the stage area were three large wooden tanks marked Novice, Intermediate, and Open. Decoys floated in the tanks, and three men studied them intently, sometimes gently turning one bird or another with a stick that resembled a pool cue. Attendants stood by with white towels to gently blot each bird dry after it emerged from the water.

Flanking the tank area were two sets of bleachers, filled to capacity. Now and then, when it was apparent that a winning bird had been selected, a cheer would go up from a certain section.

During the day announcements of winners were made on the public address system: "The winner in novice class, best diving duck, Chippy Woodwing of Ducktail, Louisiana." More cheers.

"Who's winning?" I asked a man wearing an official Ward Foundation badge.

He gave me a funny look. "Who's winning what?" he asked.

After about an hour it became clear to me that bird carving competitions are a lot like the British game of cricket. The rules are apparent only to those who are playing the game. Only after attending several competitions and studying the rules did I begin to make sense of it all.

Competition rules vary somewhat from show to show, but I'll try in this chapter to give you a general idea of how the game is played. If you plan to enter a competition, get a copy of the rules well in advance and study them carefully. That way you'll enter your bird in the proper category and at the correct skill level, and you'll avoid having an entry disqualified over some minor infraction.

Bird carving competitions are actually a series of many contests for people of varying degrees of skill. As I mentioned in the introduction, most competitions feature three skill levels: novice, intermediate, and open.

The novice class is considered the entry level in competitions. Most carvers begin here, then after winning a few blue ribbons and honing their skills move up to intermediate. After winning a few ribbons in intermediate, a carver moves on to open, which is considered the highest level.

Some competitions have other skill levels. The Ward competition has its World level, in which carvers

The major carving competitions attract large crowds and hundreds of entries. Most competitions include several different skill levels, so carvers compete with others of the same proficiency.

The audience watches as judges inspect entries in the decorative decoy category. Even though the decoys are not intended for the duck blind, they must float in a lifelike manner.

At the Ward competition, floating decoys are judged in tanks in the foreground, while entries in the decorative lifesize category are displayed on the stage.

vie for the title of world champion in five different styles of carving: decorative lifesize wildfowl, floating decorative lifesize waterfowl pair, decorative miniature wildfowl, interpretive wood sculpture, and shootin' rig.

The Ward Foundation presents purchase awards and world championship rings to each of the five winners, and the winning carvings go on display at the

Ward Museum in Salisbury, Maryland. The purchase awards vary from $20,000 for the best in decorative lifesize to $3,500 for the best shootin' rig.

Many competitions have skill levels tailored to youth, and some have senior divisions.

Once you've determined your skill level, you decide which category of competition to enter. Competition organizers are trying valiantly to make the contests as democratic as possible and accommodate as many carving styles as they can. Here are some of the major categories:

Decorative Lifesize Wildfowl—This category includes any species of wildfowl and usually depicts one or more birds in some type of environment. Emphasis is on accuracy, artistry, and innovative presentation. The birds usually are highly detailed and realistic.

Decorative Miniature Wildfowl—Similar to the above, but entries are limited in size. Some contests specify eight inches maximum, others say no more than half lifesize. Again, these entries are highly detailed and accurate, and points are given for innovative presentation.

Floating Decorative Lifesize Waterfowl—Entries are waterfowl only; most competitions designate the species. Emphasis is on detail and accuracy, and the birds are judged while they float in a tank of water.

Interpretive Wood Sculpture—This is a free-for-all category in which nearly anything goes, as long as the entries are made of wood and depict a bird of some sort. Sculptural qualities and craftsmanship win points here. Emphasis is on innovation and unique presentation.

Gunning Decoys—Traditional birds made for the duck blind. Rules vary according to the competition. Some allow texturing and extensive detail; others want only "smoothies." The International Wildfowl Carvers Association (IWCA) was formed several years ago to standardize rules governing gunning decoy contests, and many of the competitions around the country adhere to IWCA guidelines.

Most organizers try to have contests in as many categories as they can think of. Many competitions, especially in the Midwest and other areas where fish

Decorative lifesize entries usually include one or more birds depicted in some sort of environment. This peregrine falcon by Greg Woodard is presented simply, perched atop a native rock.

Most competitions have categories for decorative decoys or decoy pairs. In keeping with the decoy making tradition, the carvings are judged as they float. These mergansers by Chris Bonner won the Ward World Championship in 1989. *(Dan Williams photo)*

carving is popular, have categories for decorative fish and fish decoys. There are contests for feather carving, head whittling, painting, pyrographic art, and photography; some competitions even offer prizes for best retail display. Check out the rules brochure to determine the categories that best match your interests.

Contests within Contests

It should be noted that most competitions offer prizes not only for the best entry in, let's say, decorative lifesize wildfowl, but also for best species and best group of species (shorebirds, songbirds, and so on).

It works like a playoff system in which you advance from one level to the next. Under the Ward competition rules, the decorative lifesize wildfowl category includes six subcategories: waterfowl, shorebirds, upland game birds, birds of prey, seabirds, and songbirds. Perhaps you enter a black and white warbler in the songbird subcategory and it wins a blue ribbon as best songbird. You then compete against the five other subcategory winners for the title of best in show.

In the decorative lifesize floating waterfowl category, thirty species are eligible, and there are three subcategories: puddle ducks, diving ducks, and geese and confidence decoys. So if your black duck wins best of species, it then competes with the mallards,

Decorative miniature carvings follow most of the guidelines of the lifesize category but have maximum size limitations. Some contests specify half-size, others impose an eight-inch maximum. These robins by Peter Kaune of Washington won the Ward World Championship in miniatures.

One of the leading carvers of miniatures today is
Gary Yoder of Maryland. This great blue heron
won a first in the open division at the Ward.

teals, gadwalls, etc. for the title of best puddle duck. If it triumphs at this level, it then goes against the diving ducks and geese for the title of best in show.

If your black duck wins it all, it will have three blue ribbons around its neck: one for best in species, one for best marsh duck, and one for best in show. Small wonder that show organizers complain about budgets for awards and ribbons.

The competitions provide a forum for as many carving styles as possible, whether your interest is in decoys, decorative ducks, hawks, shorebirds, songbirds, or free-form interpretive sculpture. Get a copy of the rules, pick the category that's right for you, and go for it.

Judging open class mallards at the Ward are Paul Johnsgard, left, and Jim Sprankle.

This gadwall drake by Jett Brunet shows tremendous detail and painting skill; in addition, the bird is depicted in a graceful, pleasing pose. All of these qualities are necessary when competing at the highest levels. *(Dan Williams photo)*

Competition among carvers of gunning decoys is stronger than ever. Most contests have gunning decoy, or shootin' stool, categories, and the International Wildfowl Carvers Association has been formed to standardize rules. Here judges discuss the merits of diving duck entries.

Gunning decoy competitions usually specify a minimum of carved detail and fragile parts, yet the best carvings are elegant and graceful birds, like this pintail drake by Jimmie Vizier of Louisiana. *(Dan Williams photo)*

This nicely painted wigeon drake won the 1990 Ward competition for shootin' stools for Tom Christie of Marion, Ohio.

J. B. Garton's black duck decoy is simple and straightforward, but a beautiful bird.

One of the fastest growing categories of
competition is the interpretive division, in which
works are judged solely on artistic merit. Dave and
Mary Ahrendt of Minnesota used a combination of
paint and bare wood to convey the feeling of
speed in this sculpture of a peregrine stooping on
a swift.

This close-up shows the detailed head of the falcon, with the painted areas gradually blending into wood.

A minimum of detail is all that's needed to capture the terror of the prey bird.

This tern, carved in walnut by the Ahrendts,
seems to be swooping down to make a dive.

John T. Sharp of Ohio has won numerous prizes for his sculpted birds, such as these waterfowl carved from a single piece of walnut.

Martin Gates of Florida uses a variety of wood to carve birds native to his area. This heron with turtle, carved from walnut, is highly stylized, with sweeping lines.

A close-up of Martin's heron shows the graceful
sweep of the neck and the crest.

Some competitions offer feather carving contests,
in which the entrant carves and paints a wooden
feather and displays it with the real thing. Can you
pick out Jim Sherman's wooden grouse feather?

Head carving contests are included in some
competitions. This great blue heron head was
carved by Jack Szolis of Wexford, Pennsylvania.
(J. P. Kaufman photo)

Competitions offer contestants various skill levels
from which to choose. This barn owl was a winner
in novice class for Richard Finch of Texas, who
now has gone on to open level. *(Bill Warner photo)*

Leo Osborne of Joseph, Oregon, is one of the most prolific and eclectic wildfowl sculptors working today. Leo enjoys working with emerging forms and often carves burlwood. This sculpture of a bald eagle is titled *Song of the Pacific Northwest.*

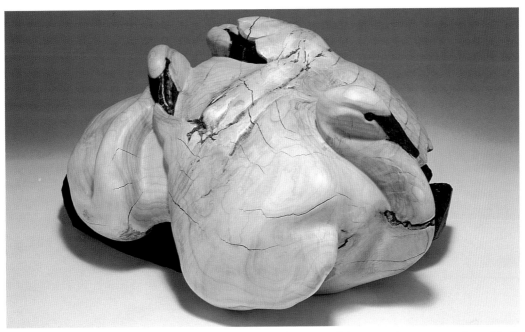

Leo's 1993 sculpture of trumpeter swans is called *Three Muses.* Carved from a pine burl, it was entered in the 1993 Ward World Championship interpretive division.

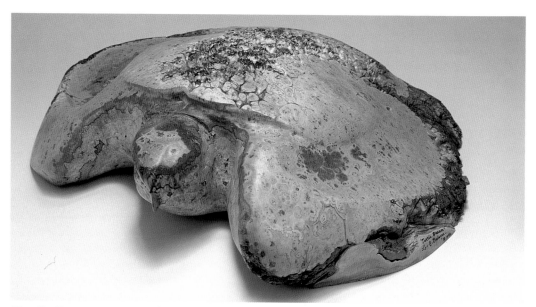

Turtle Dream, carved from a thirty-eight-inch maple burl, illustrates Leo's fascination with all wildlife. His recent work includes birds, lions, otters, and human figures.

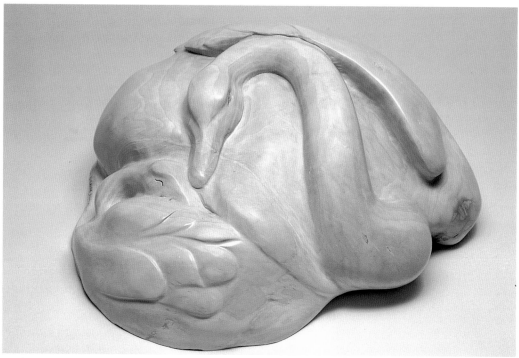

This 1992 sculpture entitled *Swan Dream* was carved by Leo Osborne from a large pine burl.

3

Judging

Wildlife art is not like baseball, where the winner is the team with the most runs after nine innings. Would that it could be so simple.

At first glance it seems incongruous. Most bird carvers are adamant about being considered artists, yet they subject their work to a judging process whose rules, some feel, enforce a sameness of presentation and execution. We like to think of art as an abrogation of rules, the product of a creative process that thrives on freedom of spirit and action. Why, then, should we limit artists by binding them with rules? Why should artists need to compete with one another at all?

Tough questions. Indeed, competitions are not for everyone, but they have many positive aspects, as conversations with the artists in chapter 1 illustrated. And rules are necessary, but most competition organizers work tirelessly to ensure that rules encourage artists to do their best work, not limit their imaginations or techniques.

The concept of carving competitions began with decoy making, when carvers' rigs were floated in tanks and the judges' task was to decide which carving would be the most effective in a hunting situation. In the early 1970s the competitions evolved to include so-called mantel birds, or decorative carvings, which had no function other than to look nice to the human eye. Rules changed to accommodate this new category of carving, but they still carried the spirit of the decoy days, which meant that if you intended to carve a cedar waxwing, then the danged thing had best look like a real cedar waxwing.

Today's competitions are still governed by the spirit of the hunting decoy. Highly realistic decorative

Waterfowl carvings never intended for the duck blind are still judged in the decoy tradition: floating in a tank of water.

waterfowl carvings, valued at $10,000 or more and never intended to go near a duck marsh, are still judged as they float in tanks of water. Some of the top competitions are considering eliminating this requirement, especially since most competitions have a separate category just for hunting decoys, which are judged in the traditional manner—floating on water, viewed from a distance; it's the overall effect that's important, not the perfection of every feather.

The issue of whether wildfowl carving is "fine art" is probably a futile question and one best left to future generations. Certainly not everything that passes through the entry tables at a competition automatically qualifies as art, but I have the feeling that the work of some carvers will still be viewed with appreciation a century from now.

On one level, carving competitions are a contest to see who can carve the most realistic bird and present it in a way that is fresh and appealing. The emphasis is on realism, craftsmanship, accuracy, and artistry. In other words, no matter how visually exciting a work is, it had better be biologically correct. To quote the 1993 Ward competition rules:

> Is the bird the right size? Are the feathers the right shape? Is the coloration and pattern correct? Are the eyes properly placed? Do the toes have the right number of joints and are they in the right places?

("Whew. Check the toes on that great blue heron, Roy. Looks like he's been playing soccer with a cinder block.")

To their credit, competition organizers are easing up a bit on the every-feather-in-its-place requirement. Artistry is encouraged within the framework of biological accuracy, and in the fast-growing interpretive categories carvers are encouraged to try anything as long as a bird is involved.

Competitions are stretching themselves to accommodate two distinct spheres: the tradition of decoy

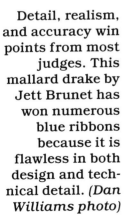

Detail, realism, and accuracy win points from most judges. This mallard drake by Jett Brunet has won numerous blue ribbons because it is flawless in both design and technical detail. *(Dan Williams photo)*

making where realism is paramount, and the freedom of expression that comes from experimentation and breaking rules. At most competitions decoy carvers and art school graduates happily rub elbows, each appreciating the work of the other but preferring to go his own way. Competition organizers are encouraging this attitude.

"Rules are necessary for the judging process—you have to have certain guidelines—but if things become too regimented and get bogged down with a lot of dos and don'ts, this can have a negative effect," says Floyd Scholz. "I feel that competition in anything is healthy because it urges one to constantly strive for improvement. When I finish a piece, I'm always eager to get feedback from my contemporaries."

Floyd says that one of the dangers of competitions is they often encourage carvers to emulate styles of those who have won. "Everyone loves a winner," he says, "and what has happened in the past is that if a particular style dominates the competitions, other carvers try to copy the style so they can win too. Sadly, the trend lately has been to keep it simple and tight,

This close-up of a Jett Brunet gadwall shows the intricacies of detail and the subtleties of painting. *(Dan Williams photo)*

This goshawk by Greg Woodard is a good example
of artistry within the framework of biological
accuracy. Greg is a falconer and is an expert on
birds of prey. *(Dan Williams photo)*

almost porcelainlike. Give the judges less to look at and they'll have less to find wrong."

Ernie Muehlmatt suggests that perhaps the rules should be loosened, placing less emphasis on detail. "If an artist can portray the essence of a bird with good design and color, it should win," he says. "John Scheeler's birds didn't look as good close-up as they did six feet away. That's the way pieces should be looked at."

Still, the bottom line in most carving competitions is accuracy. Judges want an artistic presentation—something that will excite the eye—but the bird must be lifelike and the technical skills must be there.

"The most common problems for beginning carvers are a lack of technical skill and mistakes in anatomy," says Ernie, who has judged competitions around the country for many years. "A lot of carvers have good artistic ideas, but they don't have the technical skills and anatomical knowledge to pull it off. Most carvers can't see their own mistakes, so judging helps there. I have birds I did fifteen or twenty years ago, and they're awful. But I thought they were great at the time. The key is that you have to do a lot of birds, and each has to be better than the last."

Most of the leading professional carvers also serve as judges, usually in the novice or intermediate class or in categories they do not enter. Most agree that selecting one bird over another is complex, and scoring is difficult. Says Larry Barth: "My dilemma when judging comes when I have two birds in front of me—one is technically good but boring, and the other is exciting to look at but rough. You want to give the latter carver credit, but the skills are not up to the idea. Then you have the bird carved in a carving class; you can't fault it technically, but you know it's a class bird. I like to see birds whose roots I can't trace. I like to see carvers think for themselves. When I'm judging, I lean heavily toward the product of independent thought rather than something carved from a pattern book or in a class."

Leo Osborne suggests that carvers not take the judging process too seriously. "Each judge has his own viewpoint and opinion, and the judge's background, knowledge, and perceptions help determine whether he'll select your bird over someone else's. So

Another combination of good design and technical excellence—a Cooper's hawk by Greg Woodard. *(Dan Williams photo)*

don't let it get to you too much. I've seen people walk away from competitions and put their carving tools away. You can't wrap your whole life up in whether you win or lose."

A carver's approach to judging, and being judged, often depends on the category he or she is entering. Accuracy and realism are paramount in classifications such as decorative decoy pairs, which not only must float properly but must also be of proper size and have the correct feather detail, color, and attitude. "There's a lot more nit-picking going on in decoy judging, where all you have is a bird sitting on the water," says Jett Brunet, a champion carver who frequently serves as a judge. "The judges spend much more time going over sizes and shapes and colors. In the lifesize category there is more to look at. You have bases and habitat and more complicated design, so you have a little more freedom and don't have to be as precise."

But even carvers of traditional floating decoys are being encouraged to stretch their limits creatively, says Jett. "I think the competitions have come a long way in judging decoys in recent years. As carvers got more accurate and closer to the live bird—which is what the judges looked for all along—then we needed to go to the next level and be more creative. For a while carvers stuck to simple birds done very accurately, because there wasn't a lot for the judges to pick on and you wouldn't make as many mistakes. But if you could make a preening bird and do it accurately, or one with a wing extended, you had an advantage over a simpler bird. Competitions forced us to become more accurate, and by becoming more accurate we became more daring."

Jim Sprankle began his career as a decoy carver, winning dozens of blue ribbons for floating birds, but his more recent efforts have been in decorative lifesize, where the birds can be portrayed in flight, amid habitat, or interacting with other birds or animals. "Creating something that looked like a decoy day after day, year after year, didn't interest me," he says. "I know there are some carvers who are very successful who never move the head more than thirty degrees left or right, and if they can carve that kind of bird and be happy, that's the thing to do. But I enjoy being creative, and I enjoy doing birds in flight, working out the

This hooded merganser hen by Sina Pat Kurman shows excellent detail and painting technique. *(Dan Williams photo)*

composition and trying to get the whole thing to work with as little distraction as possible. I think judging sometimes inhibits us because we're afraid that if we do something unusual the judge is going to say that the bird couldn't do that. But at this point in my life I'm going to carve what I want to carve, not what I think a judge may or may not want to see."

Sprankle is frequently a judge himself, mainly of floating decoys, so he can speak from both points of view. He says the mistake he sees most in the work of beginning and intermediate carvers is a lack of research and the resultant mistakes in anatomy. "Carvers need good reference material, because accuracy is essential," he says. "This might mean photographs, taxidermy specimens, live birds, or videotapes. I see a lot of mistakes in painting, which is the hardest part for most people. When I'm judging, I look

Jim Sprankle's sculpture of three green-winged teals with cordgrass was second in the Ward World Championship in 1993.

A close-up of Jim Sprankle's hen teal shows intricate detail and accuracy. At the highest levels of competition, carvings must display both artistry and precision.

for areas in different birds where I have trouble myself. I've carved most of the North American waterfowl over the years, and I've done a lot of research and have twenty-some species in my aviary, so I have a pretty good idea of what I'm looking at and looking for. I know I have trouble with the breasts of hen birds, with all the different feathers going different directions, so that's one of the things I look for when I judge."

The dilemma of most judges is weighing technical skill and accuracy against the more sculptural considerations of line and form. Some judges put more emphasis on technique and accuracy, others lean toward the more visual aspects of a carving. Jett Brunet often judges novice and intermediate categories, and he says he's a little more lenient when judging the work of less experienced carvers. "You don't expect to find the technical skills of open-level carvers in novice and intermediate categories, so I don't nit-pick as much. If a bird really stands out technically, then it has an appeal, but I think of myself as a sculptor, and I look for those qualities in pieces I judge. I look for good flow lines, something creative, just a good bird you can enjoy looking at for a long time. You can tell when a carver is using his own thought process and developing his own ideas. I think that's more valuable than a carver who does a great job at detailing and painting but who made the bird from someone else's pattern."

If we could come up with a consensus formula for success in carving competitions, it would probably go something like this:

1. Learn the technical skills through carving seminars, videotapes, and books, but apply them to your own ideas and motivations. Wean yourself from attempting to create clones of instructors' carvings.
2. Spend a lot of time watching live birds and learn their habits. Study photos, videotapes, and taxidermy specimens.
3. Teach yourself to be creative, or at least work on basic visual and sculptural qualities. Take classes in design, sculpting, or drawing.
4. Don't take the judging process too seriously, but try to learn something from each competition you enter. Ask the advice of more experienced carvers and judges.

Larry Barth judging at the Ward competition. The dilemma for judges, he says, comes when they encounter a bird that is visually exciting but poorly done technically.

Jim Sprankle's 1988 sculpture *Hasty Departure* captures a pair of black ducks in flight.

Startled Sprig, carved by Jim Sprankle in 1989, represents a departure for him in that the pintail is mounted on a curved base instead of in a realistic setting.

Sprankle continued experimenting with man-made
environments in this 1990 green-winged teal
sculpture, *Red River Rockets.*

Pintails over the Choptank was carved by Jim
Sprankle in 1992.

Judging the interpretive category centers more on artistry than on detail. These quail by Dave and Mary Ahrendt have little detail, but the sculpture successfully conveys the feeling of a covey rise. *(Dan Williams photo)*

Judging miniatures are, from left, Dr. Kenneth Parkes, Dr. Barry Walker, and Bob Ptashnick. In most competitions, the decisions are made by a panel of three judges, who may be carvers, painters, art experts, or ornithologists.

Floyd Scholz at work on an eagle in his studio in Vermont. Competition is healthy, he says, because it encourages carvers to do better work.

An osprey carved from pecan holds a fish whose form is emerging from raw wood. This Martin Gates work captures the osprey's catch with a minimum of detail.

Two-time world champion Jett Brunet is all smiles
while he waits for a TV interview to begin at the
Ward competition. As carving technique has
improved, artists have become more creative, he
says.

4

The Extra Edge

If there were such a thing as a simple formula for winning bird carving competitions, it would go like this. First, totally master the techniques of carving and painting. Then study and observe the bird you intend to carve until you know every nuance of color, anatomy, and behavior. And finally, include the bird in a presentation that is visually exciting, unique, and without fault in composition.

As with many simplified formulas, this one is easier stated than mastered. Yet most of the championship winners have all of these qualities, and even if such mastery may seem out of reach, it is a worthy goal. Settle for no less.

It is no coincidence that most carving competitions, in explaining judging criteria, emphasize craftsmanship, accuracy, essence of species, and artistry. In the Ward World Championship rules brochure, these four qualities are printed in bold type. And the qualities do not stand alone. "All four criteria are important," says the Ward brochure. "They all overlap and build on each other. In order for a piece to reach its fullest potential it must succeed in all four areas simultaneously."

There you have it. Where are you going to display the trophies and ribbons?

Beginning or intermediate carvers sometimes feel that there is a shortcut to success, a quick way to avoid the tremendous time that must go into mastering technique or learning about birds. Tan Brunet, the famous Louisiana carver, complains that beginning carvers come to his shop, watch him at work, and expect to go home and be able to rough out a bird with a

Larry Barth advises carvers to pay particular attention to the face of the bird. That's where the personality is, he says. This red-tailed hawk by Phil Galatas illustrates the point.

hatchet with the same dexterity. They don't realize that Tan has spent more than twenty years refining those skills. They can't be learned in a weekend of seminars.

As Ernie Muehlmatt says, carvers simply have to carve enough birds, and make enough mistakes, before they can expect to get it right.

Most professional carvers recommend that beginners attend workshops with experienced carvers. That's the quickest way to learn about the various tools and techniques. But avoid the trap of trying to carve clones of your teacher's work. Study art and design. Study birds. Go to museums. Once you develop the dexterity needed for carving and painting, get the creative juices flowing. "A good carving should tell a story," says Ernie Muehlmatt. "You can't just carve a bird and set it on a stump. There has to be a story and good design as well as flawless workmanship. It has to grab you."

Larry Barth likens carving technique to learning a language. "You want to tell a story, but first you have to learn the vocabulary," he says. "You want to get to the point where the technical skills become second nature; then you can concentrate on what you have to

Craftsmanship, accuracy, essence of species, and artistry combine to produce winning carvings, and those are the criteria used by most competitions. This scarlet tanager by Larry Barth demonstrates that the formula works.

say. Creativity is much more difficult than technique because it is conceptual. The execution is easy, but coming up with the great ideas and new ways of presenting them is difficult. Most carvers reach a point where they may still struggle some with technique but it is no longer their primary concern. The emphasis is no longer on how, but on what."

Larry often judges in the novice and intermediate ranks, and he advises carvers to study bird anatomy as well as work on their skills with a knife or burning pen. "Specifically, primary feathers are a trouble spot. People fall into an out-of-sight-out-of-mind trap. Ninety-five percent of a bird's feathers are out of sight, but you have to consider them—their point of origin and the way they lie under the visible feathers. And carvers should pay a lot of attention to the face of the bird. That's the focus, where the look is. The part of the bird that isn't feathers makes the impression."

Improving in All Areas

Jett Brunet says he strives to make each carving better than the last. "Each time I start a new project I make a real effort to improve every aspect of my carving, to make it better than anything I've done before,"

The head of this black duck by Todd Wohlt captures a feeling of action.

Blackburnian warblers by Larry Barth show the
relationship between birds and the environment.
All ingredients work together to make a successful
sculpture.

he says. "This means everything from design to laying out feathers to burning detail to the painting of each stroke."

The process begins with design, Jett says. Although he has carved several decorative lifesize pieces, his specialty is decoys, and each project begins with a consideration of the attitude, or design, of the bird. "I spend a lot of time creating the pose, something with good design and good lines, but something unique. I want a design that is graceful and fluid, a bird you can look at forever and not get tired of. Once I have the design I go to the next stages of the carving process, and I make sure I do a better job than I've ever done before, whether it's carving feather detail or painting. So the process involves both creativity and technique. The concept has to be right, and the technique should be as good as I can possibly make it."

Floating to a Win

Tan Brunet has won five world championships and has judged countless decoy contests. He believes carvers should pay more attention to how a bird floats, especially if they get fancy and carve extended wings or birds in preening poses. After all, the decoys are judged as they float in tanks of water, and in most contests rules stipulate that the decoys must float in a lifelike manner.

"Flotation is a big part of making a winning bird," he says. "A canvasback should float like a canvasback, not a blue-winged teal. And the birds should show a certain character. The drake should look more dominant. If you try to do too much with the pose, you can get into all kinds of problems. You'll have a wing or the tail underwater, or the bill and eyes won't look right. I'm a traditionalist. I like carving the simple, old-style decoys where the bird is relaxed and in a comfortable position. In other words, my decoys are not going to be doing too much."

The trend, Tan admits, is toward decoys carved in more active, sometimes even acrobatic poses. He acknowledges that it's difficult for a decoy carved in a simple position to beat one carved in a more elaborate pose, assuming the technical aspects are equal. "I'm finding it harder to win now because I'm getting

These robins won the Ward World Championship for Gary Yoder.

A close-up shows the amount of time and effort Gary put into the eye area.

beaten by birds that are doing more," he says. "That part of competitions has changed in the past few years, and I'm not sure it's for the best. The judges have to be careful not to give too many points for creativity when the decoy misses out on the basics. The skills and techniques must be there."

Giving a carving an extra edge in competition is a product of hard work and study, says Tan. "Spend a lot of time studying wild birds," he advises. "Learn all you can about anatomy and color and the way wild birds act. Success is a matter of learning about the birds and then carving and painting them as well as you possibly can."

There are fewer opportunities for carvers to get creative in the decoy category, Tan says, especially when compared with the decorative lifesize birds, which don't have to float and are usually presented in some sort of habitat or interacting with other birds or animals. "There are only so many ways you can open a wing or turn a head," he says. "That's why I like the simpler birds. But if the more elaborate poses are done well, the judges have to reward the artist for it. My advice to beginners is to slow down, keep it simple, stick to basics, try to make each bird better. You have to walk before you can run. Remember, if you carve a bird with an open bill, they're going to judge the tongue and it had better be done well."

Start with Anatomy

Jimmie Vizier, Tan Brunet's friend and mentor, lives just around the bayou in Cut Off. The two learned carving from Jimmie's father and uncle, Odee and Cadis Vizier. The elder Viziers were watermen who made decoys to hunt with, or to sell or barter for other goods. Not surprisingly, Jimmie's carving career is still centered around the traditional hunting decoy intended for a duck blind. His work is simple, elegant, and always captures the essence of the bird. The carvings may not have the feather detail of decorative birds, but they are no less pleasing to the eye.

Gunning birds provide good practice for all carvers because they make you concentrate on anatomy rather than intricate detail, Jimmie says. "The first thing a carver should learn is anatomy. That's

"I spend a lot of time creating the pose, something with good design and good lines but also unique," says Jett Brunet, who demonstrates his skill with this redhead. *(Dan Williams photo)*

first-grade material in carving school. It has to be mastered. Do a simple carving that is accurate and well-done technically. Master the simple before you try carving a bird in fancy poses."

Jimmie is a frequent judge at gunning decoy competitions around the country; he says mistakes by beginning carvers usually occur in three areas—the bill, the eyes, and the body shape.

"The most common mistake I see is with the bill," he says. "In most puddle ducks the bill is the same width along its entire length, but a lot of carvers will widen the bill where it meets the head. Most species don't have that flare in the bill."

According to Jimmie, the second most prevalent error is spacing the eyes too far apart, and the third is carving the body narrow and not rigging it to float properly. "You see birds that are too narrow fairly often, but you seldom see one that is too wide," he says.

Jimmie has been entering and winning competitions for decades, and he still finds it exciting and rewarding. As he puts it, "Competitions get the best out of you. When you put your carvings out there with the best in the country, you want to do your best."

Carvers from Bayou Lafourche have done well in carving competitions since the 1950s, when Cadis Vizier first boxed up a few of his hunting decoys and sent them to New York for the U.S. Nationals. They came back wearing ribbons, and the Cajuns have been a force in the carving world ever since.

"There was a small item in the New Orleans *Times-Picayune* about the competition, and some of Cadis's friends persuaded him to enter," Jimmie says. "He sent several carvings by mail and was surprised to find that he had won."

Jimmie, at age sixty, has been carving gunning birds for about half a century: "I liked to hang around my father and uncle when they were carving, and pretty soon I started making my own. When I was in my teens I was making hunting rigs."

The Carving as Signature

The work of Leo Osborne is eclectic and sometimes unexpected—ranging from wall hangings to forms emerging from burlwood—but when you see one of his carvings at a competition or exhibition, there is little doubt that it is Leo's work. Some undefinable style about it marks the piece as uniquely his. He calls it his signature.

"Carvers need to develop a style, a signature, that is their own," he says. "We all have ways of signing our name that become familiar and identifiable. Once you find that style, you stick with it and it becomes a symbol more than a signature. In carving, you need to develop your art to where it becomes a symbol of you. It's a difficult thing to do, especially in the decorative categories, because you can look at a whole table of birds at a competition and they all look alike. Only a few people have such a symbolic way of carving and painting that you can pick their work out of a crowd."

The danger for beginning carvers, Leo says, is the ease with which they can unwittingly adopt the style of a carver they have studied with or whose work they admire. Then, instead of being on their way to developing their own signature, they are making carvings that look like imperfect copies of someone else's work.

Leo advises carvers to develop their own style, and then to combine creativity and technique to improve their work and give it that extra edge. "Taking a carving to a higher level is a combination of a lot of things," he says. "In the interpretive category, the wood you use has a lot to do with your work, whether it's a piece of stump wood, a burl, or a laminated configuration of wood. Carvers need to learn that the wood speaks for itself and it must speak as fully as it can to give credibility to the work.

"We need to do a lot of research, to keep our eyes wide open," he says. "We need to go to museums, to see what is being done and what has been done. And by research I don't mean just in natural history, but to see what has taken place in art around the world over the centuries. Bird art is not a new medium. Study how avian art has been treated through the centuries—what the Egyptians did, the Babylonians, the Chinese, the Asian and Indian cultures. All of this is relevant to what we're doing today. It can open us up to different techniques, to ways we can adapt materials and tools we are using now to ideas that preceded us."

Leo urges carvers to take chances with their work, to experiment endlessly and not worry about whether the work will be accepted by the public or by competition judges. "If you love it, if it turns you on and you feel strongly about it, then maybe everybody else will. That's the only barometer you should go by."

Detail of a gadwall drake by Jett Brunet. *(Dan Williams photo)*

Gadwall by Rich Smoker of Maryland.

Tan Brunet, a five-time world champion, calls himself a traditionalist. He likes to carve birds in simple settings, like this bluebill.

"Carvers should start by mastering the basics," advises Tan, who judges here with Dan Brown, left, and Pat Godin.

Jim Sprankle, left, and Jimmie Vizier judge pintails as the decoys float in a tank. Carvers need to concentrate on making their decoys float properly, says Tan Brunet.

5 Case Study

In the 1992 Ward World Championship, Greg Woodard of Brigham City, Utah, won first place with a sculpture of a female kestrel on a cactus. The title of the piece was *Cactus Flower.*

The second-place finisher that year was Floyd Scholz of Hancock, Vermont, who had carved a red-tailed hawk clutching a copperhead snake.

Third went to Ernie Muehlmatt of Springfield, Pennsylvania, for his carving of a group of immature prairie falcons.

In preparing this chapter I talked with the three artists and other carvers and observers to get an idea of what makes a winning carving. It's obvious, first of all, that all three of the pieces are excellent, and with a different set of judges the distribution of ribbons might have been different. After all, judging work at this level is a subjective process. The technical aspects of the carvings are superlative, so the decision is based largely on the tastes, experiences, and eyes of the beholders, who in this case were artists Guy Cohleach and Bill Koelpin and collector Doug Miller.

I might mention that the decision created something of a controversy, because in 1992 the Ward competition rules stated that decorative lifesize entries should be "two or more birds . . . or a bird(s) interacting with another subject." Many felt that this meant that two or more birds, or a bird and another live critter, were mandatory. But a literal interpretation of the rules indicates only that a bird has to be interacting with another subject, and in the case of Greg's kestrel, the judges felt that the bird was interacting with its environment, which was a major ingredient in the work.

So what can we learn from looking at these three dramatic pieces? That it's time to sell the carving tools and take up scuba diving? No, even Greg, Floyd, and Ernie were novices once. They worked hard, did not despair, and learned from their failures, and now they are doing work that is . . . well, absolutely fantastic. Maybe one day, if we keep on working at it . . .

Let's open the discussion.

Greg Woodard: "I try to keep my carvings all one piece, but a cactus is so segmented that it seemed to make sense to make it in sections. I love cacti and the desert, and I wanted to put them all together. I've been trying to bring the western influence into my work, and I had just bought a piece of land that had a lot of cacti on it that were starting to bloom, so that's how I came up with the name. I had always wanted to do a kestrel in that position, with the outside feather pulled around. I did a drawing and my friends liked the piece, but when I thought about entering it in the World I worried about the two-bird/interaction rule and considered adding a lizard or something to it, but it just didn't work that way. I'm glad I didn't do it. It would have served no purpose."

Ernie Muehlmatt: "All three of the pieces that won in 1992 tell a story. Greg's kestrel had super design, and the preening pose of the kestrel, to me, said she was sprucing up for the first run of the day. Floyd's red-tailed hawk was defiant, proudly displaying the copperhead. In my piece, *Flight School*, I tried to give each bird a different personality: afraid, confident, curious, like they were watching Mom and Dad give them flight lessons. All three pieces had good design and flawless technical work. That's what it takes."

Greg: "I like the fact that Ernie carved his entry from one piece of wood. It forces you to be more sculptural when you do that. I love the way he designed it, the way the birds are presented. With Floyd's piece, I like the concept, and I like the bird itself."

Floyd Scholz: "I feel that Greg has explored new territory with his kestrel. It has tremendous animation and energy and is truly viewable from all angles. It's nice to see an artist rewarded for taking a chance. My only critique is that it is a bit too monochromatic—

Greg Woodard's kestrel took first place in the 1992 Ward World Championship. He included the cactus to bring a western influence to the piece.

a brown bird, brownish green cactus, brown base. I take my hat off to Greg for creating such a beautiful work of art."

Jett Brunet: "Each had a nice, fresh appeal. The kestrel had particular appeal to me, a great design and composition and color scheme. Greg has a special way of applying paint and using colors. I thought it was fantastic. Each piece had a special quality about it, and I can see why they placed where they did."

Floyd: "Ernie pulled off a remarkable achievement when you consider that this entire piece was sculpted from one block of wood. Ernie is a good friend, and my respect for him as an artist knows no bounds. Each falcon has its own personality, and even the subtle differences in age can be seen. The work has a distinct front, which makes in-the-round viewing a bit difficult. Ernie's efforts continue to inspire and influence a whole new generation of carvers. If a beginning carver were in search of a master to follow, Ernie Muehlmatt would be my first choice."

Floyd: "I felt pleased overall with my piece, *Counterstrike.* I spent a tremendous amount of time on the face and open mouth of the hawk as well as on the feet. These are areas often overlooked. In an effort to add tension and drama I chose a copperhead snake as the prey item because of its potentially lethal attributes. In addition, the light-phase southeastern copperhead's cryptic patterning and rich copper color nicely balance the hawk's deep brown and rust color.

"While researching snakes for this piece I learned that a snake's nervous system can cause the tail to twitch for up to three hours after death. I wanted to convey this sense of movement, so I borrowed an old cartoonist's trick of drawing in several forms to illustrate motion, which accounts for the additional tails carved into the base."

Counterstrike by Floyd Scholz, which finished second in the Ward World Championship for decorative lifesize carvings in 1992, demonstrates a successful overall composition. The carving has balance and color harmony, and it combines the abstract with the real. Floyd borrowed a cartoonist's trick and included multiple tails on the snake to illustrate motion. *(Tad Merrick photo)*

Close-up of the hawk's right foot shows the similarity between reptile and raptor, says Floyd. Painting feet and legs requires a different strategy from painting soft feathers, he says. "I highlight the lighter tops of the scales last. To make things interesting, I also deeply embedded the inside front toe and talon into the snake's throat to reassure squeamish viewers that the snake is in fact dead." *(Tad Merrick photo)*

Head, eyes, and open mouth combine to make this relatively small area one that demands a lot of time, research, and detail. Notice the veins in the lower area of the tongue and the drop of saliva on the tip of the tongue. *(Tad Merrick photo)*

Ernie Muehlmatt named his third-prize winner
Flight School—a group of immature prairie
falcons seems to be watching the parents give
flying lessons.

About the Author

Curtis Badger has written widely about wildfowl art, wildfowl hunting, and conservation issues in general. His articles have appeared in many national and regional magazines, and he has served as editor of *Wildfowl Art Journal,* which is published by the Ward Foundation. He is the co-author of *Painting Waterfowl with J.D. Sprankle, Making Decoys the Century-Old Way,* and *Barrier Islands.* He lives in Onancock, Virginia.

Other Books of Interest to Bird Carvers

How to Carve Wildfowl
The masterful techniques of nine international blue-ribbon winners.
by Roger Schroeder

How to Carve Wildfowl Book 2
Features eight more master carvers and the tools, paints, woods, and techniques they use for their best-in-show carvings.
by Roger Schroeder

Waterfowl Carving with J. D. Sprankle
A fully illustrated reference to carving and painting 25 decorative ducks.
by Roger Schroeder and James D. Sprankle

Painting Waterfowl with J. D. Sprankle
Over 400 spectacular color photos illustrate this incomparable painting guide. Includes step-by-step instruction for 13 projects and color charts for exact paint mixes.
by Curtis J. Badger and James D. Sprankle

Making Decoys the Century-Old Way
Detailed, step-by-step instructions on hand-making the simple yet functional working decoys of yesteryear.
by Grayson Chesser and Curtis J. Badger

Decorative Decoy Designs
Bruce Burk's three volumes *(Dabbling and Whistling Ducks, Diving Ducks,* and *Geese and Swans)* are complete guides to decoy painting by a renowned master of the art. All three feature life-size color patterns, reference photographs, alternate position patterns, and detailed paint-mixing instructions.
by Bruce Burk

Carving Miniature Wildfowl with Robert Guge
Scale drawings, step-by-step photographs and painting keys demonstrate the techniques that make Guge's miniatures the best in the world.
by Roger Schroeder and Robert Guge

Songbird Carving with Ernest Muehlmatt
Muehlmatt shares his expertise on painting, washes, feather flicking, and burning, plus insights on composition, design, proportion, and balance.
by Roger Schroeder and Ernest Muehlmatt

For complete ordering information, write:
Stackpole Books
5067 Ritter Road
Mechanicsburg, PA 17055
or call 1-800-732-3669